PHOEBE'S PERILS

A STORY OF DOMESTIC VIOLENCE

J.L. LITTLEFIELD

ISBN 979-8-88644-231-1 (Paperback)
ISBN 979-8-88644-232-8 (Digital)

Covenant Books
11661 Hwy 707
Murrells Inlet, SC 29576
www.covenantbooks.com

To the women at Maine Correctional Center in Windham, Maine, who asked me to write this story, and to the amazing women and men, survivors and victims of domestic violence and abuse, who have shared their stories with me.

INTRODUCTION

Phoebe's Perils is a continuing story of one woman's struggle with domestic violence. Watch her travel across the world and find the person she never dreamed she could be. The perils along the way will only strengthen your view of her as a very determined individual. Maybe you will see a little bit of yourself.

AUTHOR'S NOTE

Phoebe's Perils is a story of abuse, adventure, and surprise. You'll never know where it is going and neither will I until we get there. I'm fifty-two years old, soon to be fifty-three, and this story was started when I was fifty-one years old. It was written one chapter a month with no pre-thought to its ending or process. It has been an adventure for me too. I have begun to see it as a kind of journal entry. Whatever comes to mind comes through my pen to the page. To make things accurate, I have often had to return to earlier chapters. The facts in Brazil were from a trip I took there in 1997 and are as accurate to that time as possible. The actual abuse issues are part of mine and of others whom I have grown to respect and love. This book is a journey. Take it with care.

CHAPTER 1

Phoebe fell down the stairs and came to rest against the wall. She felt her arms and legs and slowly straightened herself, expecting pain. She was a little sore but seemed to have nothing broken. Why, when the world seemed to be going right, could so many bad things happen to her? She had moved to Maine to get away from the bad things in her life, and yet they seemed to follow her.

Joseph had found her after just three months of peace. He said that he loved her and must have her in his life, but he threatened to control her just as he had in New York. Was there nowhere to hide? He was in the motel now, getting his stuff and coming to get her so they could return to New York and their penthouse apartment.

Phoebe thought, *I would like to say I didn't miss the life we had, but I was afraid of him. I couldn't really put my finger on it. Just a feeling of suffocation, like he somehow would drain the life right out of me. I deserved better than the constant dread of his saying something mean to me or threatening to kill me in the night when I was sleeping. What should I do? He will be here within the hour.*

The rain came down hard, and Phoebe saw the taxi approaching. She had returned to New York with Joseph and was now planning her escape—for good. This leaving and coming back had to stop. Phoebe believed she had a better chance of survival if she stayed in the city and made something of herself by herself. She was on her way to an interview with a fashion designer—work she used to do before she met Joseph. Her portfolio tucked under her arm, she left the taxi and looked up at the building holding her destination. She would hold her head up high, as her counselor had told her, and remember that she deserved this job.

CHAPTER 2

Yes, she deserved this job, but would they think so? She had prepared carefully for this job interview—just the latest fashions with matching heels, makeup, and nails done professionally as well as her hair. She wasn't crazy about the blonde highlights, but the salon guaranteed her that this easy-to-care-for style was the latest with up-and-coming professionals. She was nervous, but this was when she was at her best. Joseph had not found out yet, and she wasn't sure what she would do when he did. The makeup artist had done his best to hide the bruises, but she could still see them when she looked in the mirror. He didn't like the stroganoff she had made for dinner. It was too salty, he said. Well, maybe next time she should add a whole salt shaker full of salt. Boy, when she thought about it, she wondered if she should just kill him and get it over with. Maybe a jury would see it her way. She thought constantly of ways to do it. Mostly to kill him in his sleep because he was so strong, and this was the only time she had a chance. Maybe to kill him with poison, but how would she get it into him?

The interview went well. It was a panel of the four designers that she would be working with. The only glitch she ran into was the two-year gap in her employment history when she was on the run from Joseph. She explained it by saying that she took two years to explore her love for fashion all over the world. The truth is that she had noticed the fashions of those places, but only in a flyby manner as she was always worried that he would catch up with her. The panel ended by saying that she was a strong candidate and that they would be conducting second interviews. She would hear, either way, in the next twenty-four hours. She had given them the cell phone number on a phone that Joseph didn't know she had purchased. She set the phone on vibrate in case Joseph was with her when she got the call. She felt confident that she would get good news.

Phoebe tucked her portfolio under her arm and left the building with her head held high. She was going to a motel in the movie district of Manhattan. She didn't think Joseph knew his way around there. As she stepped to the curb, a taxi stopped, and Joseph got out and pushed her in and almost sat on her as she tried to get back out. Then she tried to get out the other side. He grabbed her wrist and pulled her back to him. *Why me?* she thought. She felt like a dog on a chain. He was talking, but she couldn't hear him. She was thinking about how she could escape. Finally, the words came through, "We're going to Paris. Taxi driver, airport please."

CHAPTER 3

The red flowers were so brilliant, she could almost smell them even though she knew they were not real. Her mind grasped at everything that passed her by, looking for someone or something to rescue her. The airport terminal wasn't very crowded, and the smell of diesel fuel drifted up to her nose. She tugged at her arm and felt Joseph's grip tighten on her elbow. No one would guess that this well-dressed, handsome man was a terrorist. How about that! She had her own personal terrorist. As they approached the gate for their departure to Paris, she asked her guardian if she could use the bathroom. She had to get away if at least for a moment. He said to make it quick and not to try anything or she would regret it. She would regret any decision she made because, until he was dead, she would always make decisions based on fear. The bathroom was cold and smelled like disinfectant. There was a young mother struggling with an infant on the changing table, making cooing noises to calm the little one. She quickly ducked into the first stall and locked it behind her. She was shaking visibly. How did she get into this position?

When she and Joseph had met three years before at the University of New York campus, she never dreamed that she would be at a New York airport heading to a country she'd never been to with a man she had grown to hate. He treated her like a queen back then. Wining and dining with her at the city's finest restaurants; playing indoor tennis with her every Saturday morning. He brought flowers to her every Friday at the law firm where she worked as a secretary. When did it happen? Sometime after they moved in together, he started monitoring her phone calls, telling her whom she could see and what she could do. She told him that she felt smothered, but he said he just loved her so much. The first time he hit her, she would never forget that night. She had stood up to him and demanded that she was going to spend a night with the girls. He hit her in the face, knocking her down to the soft carpet in the living room. She was startled. What had she done? She ran to the bathroom, locked the door, and looked at the large red mark just below her left eye. He had chased her and knocked loudly, yelling at her, "Why did you make me do that? Are you trying to ruin what we have?"

He was right. Why did she keep resisting his love? Now, she wondered, what kind of love is this? What was she doing? How can she find a way out? There was no noise in the bathroom now. She could hear the loudspeaker announcing her flight at gate 18 for Air Europe. What was the right thing to do? Why couldn't Joseph just die from a brain aneurism (a lot of people do)? If she could only just find a way out. She heard his voice at the door, "Phoebe, we need to go, NOW!" Her cell phone, the one Joseph didn't know about, began vibrating.

CHAPTER 4

The bathroom felt colder than she had noticed before. She quickly put her phone back, realizing that she had almost answered it. Some things just seemed more important right now. She listened closely to hear Joseph's voice. She knew he was not beyond coming into the women's room after her. As her heart raced, she took off her shoes, put them in her bag, and quickly climbed on top of the back of the toilet. Then she held her breath waiting. *Who was I to think I could get away from him? What was I thinking?* She heard a murmur of voices outside the door. She could hear Joseph yelling and then quiet. The door opened, and a woman's voice called out, "Are you still in here, Phoebe Miller?" She said nothing. Her heart was still in her throat. "What should I do?" She was too scared to respond. The door shut, and all was quiet except for the distant noises of the airport. She waited. She hadn't noticed before an advertisement for Varig Airlines out of Miami with daily flights to Brazil. It looked so beautiful! Peaceful! Her mind went back to her trip there when she was ten years old. She was all alone, but not alone. All the Varig Airlines staff treated her like a queen. She knew a little Portuguese from her mother. *Bom dia* meant good day. She went to see her uncle Haverson in Natal in Northeast Brazil. It was beautiful there and there were very few tourists to ruin it.

She heard the bathroom door open again. She held her breath. Another stall opened, and someone was going to the bathroom. She slowly got down off the toilet and put her shoes back on. She would probably scrub her feet for days from being in contact with the toilet. She went to the bathroom and quickly flushed. As she came out of the stall, she looked warily in all directions. She washed her hands and slowly opened the bathroom door. People seemed to be rushing everywhere. She thought with choked back tears, *If I could just go somewhere safe.* If she started crying now, there would be a flood. Joseph had destroyed her ability to stand up for herself. She drifted with the crowd and kept her head down trying not to be noticed. She heard Joseph's voice yelling, "Phoebe, stop!" She went into panic mode and started running. Now she kept her head up and looked for a way out. Ahead, they were doing the last call to board a plane connecting to Miami. She reached into her purse and took out the Paris tickets. She had an instant plan. Miami and then Brazil! She pried open the closing door and then let it shut with a slam of finality. She heard him pounding on the door, and she ran into the dark hallway leading to the plane.

The stewardess asked for her ticket, and Phoebe handed over her Paris ticket. "Ma'am, you're on the wrong plane."

"What plane am I on?" she asked innocently.

"This is a connecting flight to Miami, Florida," she offered.

"Can I still take this flight? I seem to have changed my plans."

"I can't give you a refund for the difference," she explained.

"That's okay. I have my credit card with me and can charge any additional flights."

"I can offer you first-class accommodations as that is where our empty seats are."

"That would be fine," Phoebe cheerily replied. She sat down and started biting her fingernails. Would she really get away? She had never told Joseph about her relatives in Brazil. Maybe because she had been closed off from her family for so long. Besides, her life had been meaningless. It was all about Joseph. The seatbelt light came on, and the safety film began. Her escape had begun.

CHAPTER 5

I awoke with a start. *Where am I?* I asked my beating heart. Oh! Yes! I am on my way to Brazil. The movie was *Toy Story 3* in Portuguese. Wow! My Portuguese was rusty. Where was the ten-year-old little girl who bravely conversed with other passengers she didn't even know? There was something comforting about all the Brazilian faces around her. Everyone could be Brazilian here—Chinese, Japanese, Portuguese, Europeans, and they were all native Brazilians. Not everyone had that elusive tan that some of the natives had. Her meal arrived. She couldn't remember all the names of the foods before her, but she instantly remembered what she liked and didn't like. The little green square that looked like lasagna was one of her favorites, and when the flight attendant came by, she remembered to ask for guarana juice. It was like nectar from heaven. Oh, so sweet! As she reminisced the man in the seat next to hers stirred. He looked like a native Brazilian in color, yet he was dressed like a tourist. He said, "No thank you," in English in regard to his meal and asked for a scotch and soda instead. He looked at her meal with disgust and remarked, "I don't know why they feed us this native stuff. I just want a juicy steak." She said nothing but just smiled and looked away. She really wasn't interested in getting involved in a conversation with him. He interrupted her thoughts by asking a question, "Can I switch seats with you? The window seat always gives me vertigo." She answered with the affirmative as she preferred the window seat plus it would give Phoebe the chance to look at something and gladly ignore him. The view was clear, and she could see the salt ponds on the edge of the Brazilian coastline. There were so many of them, it was possible to count them all. The red soil of the land seemed to stand out to her. She was glad that it would only be a few more hours before they touched down in Rio. Where would she go from there? She would have to stop using her credit card at some point or Joseph would just follow her wherever she went. Phoebe had only twenty-seven dollars in American money, which right now (according to the flight attendant) was equal to thirty Brazilian reals. Sometimes she was amazed that she had managed to live this long with little or no common sense.

Take for instance what had happened in the Miami airport. Joseph had followed on the next flight to Miami from Kennedy airport. She recognized him in the distance as he scoped out the entire layout of the airport. She had ducked into a shop and purchased a sunhat to hide her face. She bought a bright flower-colored hat that said, "Here I am!" She was trying reverse psychology and hoped it would work. She had been saved from recognition by a tourist—a fat lady with a flower dress and sunglasses that looked too big for her head. She asked Phoebe if she could buy her hat from her as it would perfectly match her outfit. Phoebe had said it was nothing special and that the lady could probably buy one at an airport store. The lady told Phoebe that she had checked every store and was certain there was nothing like it. Phoebe had given her the hat and said she could have it, but she insisted on paying her for it. She pressed twenty-seven dollars into her hand and said, "Thank you so much!" It was then that she had seen Joseph, and he seemed mesmerized by the flower hat and began following the hat through the crowd. She moved slowly in the opposite direction, which happened to be the direction she needed to go in for an international flight. She had to wait an hour in that hot and sticky airport for her flight to Brazil. She was hungry but assured herself she could wait. After all, she would soon be a long way from home.

CHAPTER 6

She was falling, falling, falling, then she landed at the bottom of the stairs. Bruised and beaten, hard to move. Something was on top of her. She awoke with a start and realized that she had forgotten to put up her meal table. Yes, she was still on the plane on her way to Rio, Brazil. It was a long flight from Miami, Florida. She looked out the window, and suddenly the plane appeared to just miss a mountain to her left. The green mountainside was so fresh compared to the coldness and staleness she felt in her soul. Why did she continue to get involved with men that hurt her? Before Joseph had been Jim who had thrown her around like a rag doll. She had escaped him only by a "fortunate" accident where he had been killed while skiing on the slopes in Aspen. Why couldn't Joseph just have a "fortunate" accident? She would like to say she would gladly arrange it, but the movies about prison kept her away from such wanderings in her mind. Oh! Wow! She could see the Christ the Redeemer statue in Rio. They were getting ready to land. She put up the food tray and put her seat in the upright position. What would she do now? She had no idea.

Once they landed, she quickly got her purse, bulging with stuff she knew she needed, down from the overhead luggage space. The bustle started in the plane and just continued into the airport where groups of people were either welcoming passengers or looking to sell or buy things from tourists. She had forgotten how crazy this place could be. She tried with her limited Portuguese to get thirty reals for her twenty-seven dollars. No one seemed interested at first, then everyone seemed interested. She was confused. The man from the plane grabbed her elbow and led her away from the crowd that had gathered. He said to her, "Do you know what you were saying?" She explained to him that she wanted thirty reals for her twenty-seven dollars. He laughed so loud that she looked around to see if people were watching them. "What you said was I will sell myself to you twenty-seven times for thirty reals!" She shook her head and mumbled to herself, "Why did I think that I could escape from Joseph. I am a mess!"

"Cheer up," he said. "If you are willing to sell your necklace, I can give you a really good deal."

She thought, *What would my grandmother say if she saw me now?* She had given Phoebe the necklace on her sixteenth birthday. She hardly ever took it off. It was silver and looked like a braided knot in the middle of a circle. It was supposed to mean that we were tied together for eternity. She believed it. Sometimes, she would say things, and it would seem like her grandmother was speaking. She looked at the man and said, "What is a really good deal?"

He smiled. "Well, I was thinking one hundred reals, and you could keep your twenty-seven dollars and hope to get thirty reals for them."

"I don't know," she replied. Then as if her grandmother was speaking, she said, "Only if you do the exchange of my twenty-seven dollars." They both smiled. After the exchange, she quickly, as if she had done it a thousand times, went to the ticket counter to check on a ticket to Natal where her uncle Haverson lived. The line was short, and she got to the counter before she knew what to say. She had been daydreaming. "How much is a ticket to Natal?" she asked.

The ticket agent replied with a smile, "One hundred and thirty-five reals."

Phoebe gasped. "One hundred and thirty-five reals! How come so much?" She looked down at the floor. She remembered a twenty real ticket when she was a little girl. Of course, that was a half fare.

The lady at the ticket counter became impatient. "It is the height of tourist season!" Suddenly, a five real bill landed on the floor in front of her. She looked around to see if anyone had dropped it. The place seemed empty all of a sudden. She bent to pick it up and smiled at the lady and said, "One one-way ticket to Natal, please." She had an hour to wait for her plane, and when she went to the bathroom, she made a decision that meant she would never turn back. She cut up her credit cards, every last one of them.

CHAPTER 7

The runway was ending in front of her. She cried, "Pull up! Pull up!" Then she felt the plane shudder to a stop just feet from the trees. She had arrived in Natal, Brazil, the hometown of her uncle Haverson. Would he recognize her? Had he moved? She looked around and noticed everyone calmly preparing to disembark. This near collision of the plane must be an everyday occurrence. Her heart was still racing, and she felt embarrassed that she had cried out. She held her head down and quietly and quickly got off the plane. As a child, she must have slept through the landing because she certainly would have remembered. The airport was almost deserted, just a few people milling about. She quickly went outside and got into a taxi (one of the few in the city). As she traveled the streets, she imagined Joseph following her. She still felt like she was running. The taxi stopped in front of a medium-sized villa. Her uncle was rich. This was his summer home as his winter home was in Recife. She was glad that it was summer because her uncle had told her that the rats in Recife were as big as small dogs. The taxi driver looked into the backseat where Phoebe was and smiled with his hand out. She put up her finger and said in Spanish, "*Uno momento*." She knew now that her Portuguese was so bad, so she said, "One moment," in Spanish, hoping he would understand. It was her understanding that most Brazilians understood basic Spanish phrases.

Phoebe got out of the taxi and ran to the front door. She only knocked once, and the door swung wide open and revealed a medium-built, medium-height, dark-skinned, mostly dark-haired, smiling man. He lifted her off her feet and began rattling off phrases in Portuguese. Phoebe told him, "Uncle, my Portuguese stinks, and I have to pay the taxi thirteen reals."

"Oh, what a cheap price to pay for my favorite niece!" He handed her the money, and Phoebe quickly ran down the front path to pay the man. She counted out the money, and there were twenty-three reals, and she knew her uncle was a generous tipper. She returned to the villa where he ushered her into the house. She excused herself to the bathroom and was surprised at the feminine touch. There was pink everywhere and a seashell theme to its accessories. Her mind went back to her aunt Linda, who had died when she was twelve years old. Could Uncle be married now? She supposed that was to be expected. Where was she? Would she like her? No one could compare with Aunt Linda. She heard yelling suddenly and was afraid to come out of the bathroom. The yelling was in Portuguese, so she couldn't understand it. Had Joseph followed her from the States? Would he make her go back to New York City where he could control her and abuse her? What should she do? There was a knock at the door, and she realized that she was terrified. What was up with her and bathrooms? Uncle Haverson spoke softly through the crack of the door, "Are you alright, my little bird, you've been in there a long time?"

"I'm alright, Uncle. I was just startled at all that yelling."

He laughed. "Oh! It is the stupid little dog that Maria brought here. He was out chasing the birds, and you know how I hate that. In fact, your little dog used to do that." Phoebe's breathing eased, and her fists unclasped as she reached to open the door. Uncle knew something was wrong. He looked closely at Phoebe's face and covered his mouth with his hand. "Who did this, little bird? Who did this to you?" he said this as he pointed to the bruise under Phoebe's eye.

CHAPTER 8

It was New Year's Eve, and there was a festive mood in the air. Oh! How she loved new beginnings. Christmas had been a somber event because Aunt Linda had passed away on Christmas Eve many years ago. Phoebe tried not to drink too much, mostly because drinking reminded her of Joseph and how violent he was on so many New Year's Eves. Maria, her new aunt, was so pleasant and so different from her aunt Linda. Maria was like an old couch, comfortable and down-to-earth. Aunt Linda had had a warm personality, but everything had had to be in a specific place. Phoebe was getting used to Maria now and had spent many long evenings talking to her about Joseph and how she had been running from him for so long. Her bruises on her face had finally healed, but the memory of their pain was often as fresh as the day he put them on her. The question was what would she do now? Her Portuguese was getting better every day, and the people of Natal made Phoebe feel more comfortable every day. Even the grocery clerk knew her by name. Uncle still called her little bird, and that's what she felt like—a little bird flying away from the trouble in her life. Her phone rang, and startled, she answered it quickly in English, forgetting where she was.

Tomorrow was New Year's Day. Who could be calling her this late? She immediately changed to Portuguese when she realized who it was. The man was a fashion designer in the city who was up and coming in the tourist industry. He asked her to come into his office tomorrow afternoon with her portfolio. She asked him if Thursday would be soon enough because she had a few things to put in order. He said that one o'clock would be fine. She thanked him, and after ending the call, she ran to the kitchen to tell Maria and ask her for access to her uncle's office to use his computer. She prayed, "God, help me to get this portfolio together. I need this job, and I don't want to be a burden to my uncle and his wife. Please keep me safe and show me your way. In Jesus's name, amen." Now that she felt calmer, she got a cup of coffee and locked herself in her uncle's office, determined to finish her portfolio in record time. It was late at night, and she hadn't even noticed because the office had no windows. She had drunk about ten cups of coffee since she received the call, but she was fighting to keep her eyes open. She sighed deeply as she printed the last page of her portfolio.

She was so blessed to be able to use her uncle's computer with the latest upgrades. As she paused before closing out the screen, she noticed on the main menu a file called "My Dearest Linda." Curiosity got the best of her, so she clicked on it. Patterns came before her eyes, floor plans, and then a buzzer went off loud enough to raise the dead. A warning came on the screen saying, "Security Breached." What should she do?

Her uncle appeared through the locked door and yelled above the alarm, "Reset it, reset it!" Phoebe stared at the keyboard for a second and then pressed control-alt-delete. The alarm went off, and the peaceful woodland scene screensaver came on. She looked at Uncle. He said nothing at first but stared at the floor. His phone went off, and he answered it quickly and said, "Security restored."

CHAPTER 9

Her dreams were filled with nightmares of Joseph chasing her, catching her, and beating her. She would wake up with a start and often run to the bathroom to see if he left marks. She never found the marks, but the pain of the beatings and her sore soul was just as fresh as the day, not so long ago, when that had been her only life. All that she had ever known. She often pondered about the people here in Brazil and would look at passersby wondering if someone beat them at home. Their brown skin would hide their bruises well. *Bang! Crash!* What was happening! Maria's voice could be heard from the kitchen. "Fido, come here!" It was that little dog that Maria adored. He had gotten into the garbage and knocked it over. Phoebe looked down at the mess and let out a hearty laugh. Holding her stomach, she pointed out the door at Fido chasing the birds again. Maria ran out after him yelling at him to stop. Boy, it felt good to laugh and to be part of something that wasn't life-threatening.

She had her interview with the fashion designer in downtown Natal at 1:00 p.m. today, and she was nervous. It had been three years since she had worked in the world of fashion, and although she tried to keep up, she was worried about how she might compare with others. Maria had been a big help in catching her up with local fashion, and Phoebe's travels to England and Rome gave her an advantage. Phoebe stared at a picture of Uncle and Maria with Maria's grown son, Lincoln, and wondered if she would ever have a family. It wasn't impossible, but how could she be sure that Joseph wouldn't appear and ruin everything. Enough thinking. Today required action, and she was up to the task. Phoebe quickly got dressed and had a cup of coffee and a poached egg with toast. She was ready to run a couple of errands before getting ready for her interview. On her way out the door, her cell phone rang. She looked at the number and didn't recognize it, so she didn't answer it. She had to be careful. Since being in Brazil, she had abandoned all her old numbers and bought a new phone with an unlisted number. It was worth the extra monthly charge. As she thought this through, her phone rang again, and she recognized her uncle's number immediately. She quickly answered it and gladly said, "*Bom dia*, Uncle."

He returned the salutation with a masculine, "*Bom dia*, little bird."

"What's up?"

He quietly, but firmly replied, "We need to talk about last night."

"Oh," Phoebe answered softly. He asked her what time would be good for her, and she said that after supper would be good. Uncle paused for a moment, then answered, "After 10:00 p.m. in my office."

"Okay, see you then," Phoebe replied, but a dial tone was the response. Had she made him mad? She was never sure about men. She always felt like they were either mad at her or in love with her. She felt dread in the pit of her stomach. She had to put these thoughts aside because she had errands to finish and an interview to complete. She had to get a grip on herself. The grocery store, or *supermercado*, was busy. She quickly got what she needed and approached the cashier. As she got nearer to the checkout, she stared at the man in front of her. He looked familiar. It was the way he held himself and how he walked. Suddenly, to her surprise, he turned around and looked at her and said in perfect English, "Hello, Phoebe." She just stared. It was the man from the plane that had helped her at the Rio de Janeiro airport.

CHAPTER 10

As we enter the tenth chapter of this book, I want to remind my readers that there are many resources to help you if you are or have been a victim of domestic abuse. Most of all it is important for you to know that you are not alone and there is a better way. In the US call the National Domestic Violence Hotline—1–800–799–7233. In Canada, call 211–CANADA. In Mexico, go to the website www. vidasinviolencia.inmujeres.gob.mx (if there is an emergency call 911).

*****

As she stared at the man in the grocery store, her phone rang. It was that strange number again. In an impulsive moment, she answered it, "*Bom dia, esta es* Phoebe Miller." What a relief! It was the fashion design company Aware! They wanted to know if she could come in at 2:00 p.m. instead of 1:00 p.m., and she gladly replied yes because she was mesmerized by the man in front of her. After hanging up there was an awkward moment, and then they simultaneously said, "Well," and then they both laughed.

He abruptly spoke, "Phoebe, if you remember right my name is Ralph. I have business here in Natal for a week. Would you join me for lunch at the restaurant across the street so we can talk?"

She looked around herself, thinking, then replied, "Sure, I guess I have time, but come to my place because I have to put away the refrigerated items I have bought."

"I will follow you. Lead on."

She quickly paid for her items and walked briskly across the parking lot. The morning sun was getting more intense as the afternoon approached. The restaurant would have been deserted, and she didn't want to be alone with Ralph. At least at home, Maria would be a great onlooker and listener if she was overwhelmed by this man's advances. She didn't trust men in general and wondered at herself for agreeing to eat with him and talk to him.

The traffic was heavy as people rushed to get home for their siestas. As soon as they hit the suburbs, it was as if the cars didn't exist. Mostly foot traffic was here where people returned from the bus station. As she turned onto Uncle Haverson's street, she looked in her rearview mirror, almost hoping Ralph wasn't there. What was she thinking? This is what allowed Joseph back into her life when she was running from him. She wasn't being careful enough. She would make a quick lunch of it and explain to Ralph that she was grateful for all the help he had given her in the Rio airport but that she was in good hands now. Yes, she would be firm, but polite. She pulled up to the house, and they both parked on the street. She could tell he had a rental car and that gave her some peace that he would soon be out of her life. She smiled at him and said, "Follow me." She walked quickly to the front door and opened it. The screen was open, but the door was locked. Maria only locked it when she was going to be gone a while on errands. Feeling sad now, Phoebe fished out her keys and opened the door. She led him to the kitchen, and they made sandwiches together. The chips and cola completed the feast. As they sat at the kitchen table, she felt like she was talking to an old friend. They talked about politics, world news, and the world of fashion design. Then with a start, she realized it was one thirty, and she needed to get ready for her interview. She excused herself, showed him to the door, and promised to stay in touch (after all, he was handsome and a great company). She rushed to the bedroom to change. She grabbed her portfolio and was briskly walking toward the front door when she noticed Uncle Haverson's door to his office was open. She backtracked a few steps and heard her uncle say, "I'm meeting with her tonight. I'll break it to her gently."

CHAPTER 11

Her heart was racing. She needed to calm down, or she would be an emotional wreck during this interview. She shouldn't be nervous because she knew the field of fashion, and she was far from her abuser, Joseph. She hoped it wouldn't be an all-male panel because, try as she may, men still made her nervous. She remembered what her father had told her when she had starred in the school play. She should just picture the audience in their underwear. This had often brought a smile to her lips. She smiled now at the thought of her father's hand on her shoulders as he told her this advice. She was a mere ten years old when he gave it to her. She raised her head high and confidently walked through the glass doors of Aware! She approached the desk and announced her name to the secretary. The woman smiled and directed her to the interview room on the main floor. The green carpet soothed her senses, and the wall paintings spoke of the Brazilian heritage. She had nothing to worry about. This job would be hers. What happened next took her breath away.

She opened the door to see Ralph sitting at the table. Yes, Ralph from Rio and now from Natal. His smile threatened to relax her against her better judgment. What was he doing here? As if reading her mind, he spoke, "You're probably wondering what I'm doing here, but I couldn't warn you of my presence here today because I feared you wouldn't come. I've looked over your application and am impressed with your experience and knowledge of fashion worldwide. What do you think makes you stand out as a candidate for this position?" He finished his question with a serious twist of his mouth.

She looked him straight in the eyes, with her shoulders back, and replied, "I know how to survive in the toughest of times. I am perfect for this company because I am tenacious and don't know how to give up on something I believe in. I will be committed to this new company, and I will see it succeed."

Ralph Emerson smiled. "I knew you were the one for the job. When can you start?"

"You haven't even seen my portfolio," she said in astonishment.

"I don't need to. I've seen the producer of that portfolio, and your application tells me where you've been, and our lunch told me who you are. Can you see us working together?"

She thought for a moment and stared at his cool blue eyes. Not blue in a stern way, but gentle, like the blue of a lapping ocean wave upon the shore. Comforting in a special way. "Yes," she replied. "I look forward to our new adventure."

As she approached home, she wondered what she would tell Uncle Haverson. She was walking on a cloud. Now she could be self-sufficient, and soon she would be a working woman in what she loved most, fashion. She opened the door to the house almost breathless and almost walked into Uncle Haverson, who stood only a few feet in front of her. He looked stern. "Phoebe, we need to talk about what happened the other night. Things may have to change around here because of it. I'm afraid I can't risk you being involved with my secure computer system. You will have to move out."

CHAPTER 12

"My name is Joseph. I am a peaceful person. I am a prisoner. I am an abuser. I am…" He couldn't think of anything else to write. This domestic violence class was for the birds! What was the benefit of listing a bunch of words about what he thought he was? But his case manager had explained that this class was on his case plan. What he really wanted to write was, "I am scared. I am a little boy inside. I am angry at what my parents did to me, and I am sad that I can't find Phoebe." My parents abused me terribly when I was little. I was beaten for not eating my food and beaten for eating too much. I did nothing right. I had false teeth at age twenty because my parents had knocked them all out. Now I was in prison for two years for punching out an airline official who wouldn't tell me Phoebe's destination. Violence was my life. What would I do now that I learned that this could have consequences? He slumped in his chair. The class was almost over. He had anger management in the mornings and domestic violence in the afternoons. He was glad for his martial arts training because when he got here, all he had had to do was pick some of the toughest guys and he no longer feared for his safety. Some of the biggest guys protected him from others. He got paid in commissary for protecting some of the smaller men. The instructor's voice brought him out of his thoughts. He was being asked to share what he had written. He said, "Pass," upon which the instructor said, "Joey, you can pass now and then, but if you pass all the time, you won't pass the class. If I were you, I wouldn't enjoy taking this class over and over again. It doesn't get any easier." He looked the instructor straight in the face and nodded. As he returned to his cell, he passed some officers where the female guards were gathered. He smelled a light scent of perfume, and his mind traveled back in time to when he had first met Phoebe. She smelled like that. It smelled like the earth in early spring.

Suddenly the rage rose up within him. Why did she disagree with him about his idea to go to the movies? If that had never happened, he would have never slapped her and knocked out one of her front teeth. That implant had cost him a pretty penny. At least he took care of her. She wouldn't have to have false teeth. Then there was the time she had disagreed with him about what to wear to that concert. That was bad. He had meant to just shove her, but she had cascaded down the stairs. He thought he had killed her. She was so still lying there in the middle of the staircase on the landing. His thoughts were torn. It would serve her right to die, but then what would he do with her gone? He loved her, had even thought of marrying her. His thoughts were interrupted by an inmate, whispering in his ear, "We found Phoebe. She's in Natal, Brazil, at her uncle's house."

CHAPTER 13

As she looked around her new apartment and the lovely things she had bought for it, she began to cry, sobbing uncontrollably. How could Uncle Haverson kick her out of his house just because she had opened a file on his computer? What was he into that could be more important than family? Was she still his little bird? She had had more questions than that since that day two weeks ago when he had told her to leave. She had talked to him once since then on the phone asking him to come over and see her new apartment and to bring Maria over to dinner. He had given a noncommitted, "That would be nice." It seemed that the ball was in his court now, and she would just have to wait. Patience was not one of her strengths. Especially when it came to secrets. She had always been the curious type, and she was determined to find a way to find out what her uncle was into and what was on that computer or both. She hadn't come up with a plan yet because there were so many obstacles in the way. Uncle had made it clear that she was not to come over to his house, and Maria had been no help. She had seen Maria several times in the last two weeks in the grocery store, and she had been friendly, but quiet and just said, "I don't know," to all the questions Phoebe had asked her.

Work at Aware! was going well. She had some promising designs that her boss was allowing her to send to the production line. It was a spring line of dresses that expressed the Brazilian culture. She had also designed a line of pantsuits for the colder winters in Brazil. Her favorite piece was a coral-colored pantsuit with warriors on a battlefield taking place in Natal's open country that had been cleared from the previous rainforest. She could almost smell the sea where it ended the borders of the battlefield. The rust-colored soil was a great contrast to the coral-colored background. This outfit said, "This is

Natal!" She knew she shouldn't do it, but Uncle's house was drawing her. She quickly got ready for work and glanced at the clock. If she hurried, she could catch a taxi and swing by Uncle's, just to look, and still be on time for work. She just missed the place, she was telling herself. She called the taxi company and got a busy signal. She thought, *I'm glad it was busy. I should get a taxi from the other side of town. That way if Uncle looks out the window he won't be suspicious.* She called Universal Taxi, and the dispatcher picked up on the first ring. He said it would be only ten minutes because he had a man in the area. That would work. She hurried out the door and quickly walked down in front of the apartment building. It was a beautiful day to be in Brazil. She got to his house rapidly, and as they approached the street, she could see several police cars with their roof lights flashing and an ambulance, much like a station wagon in America, was between them. As they went by in the taxi, Phoebe could see her uncle being wheeled out on a stretcher, and on the front of the house were bright red spray-painted letters spelling out one word, "Joseph."

CHAPTER 14

Phoebe was still shaking even though her mind had stilled with the knowledge that her uncle's stab wounds were superficial. Uncle Haverson had remained silent about what had happened at the house, but the scene she had come upon spoke for itself. There was a broken front door, blood splatters on the floor leading from the kitchen to the front door, and blood on the hallway walls. On the floor, by the door, was a large kitchen knife covered with bright red blood. It was so nice to be in the house, and Phoebe took the opportunity to look around. Her bedroom still looked the same with the homey-looking quilt that her aunt had made. As she walked to the back of the house, she noticed that the wall in the hallway was blank in a spot where something had been. It was Uncle's office door! It was gone! Where was it, and where did it go? While she was thinking a police officer approached her and asked her in a rough voice, "What are you doing?" She quickly explained that she was looking for the bathroom. He took her by the arm and led her outside saying, "Come with me! This is a crime scene!" She rushed along with him, carefully avoiding stepping in the blood splatter.

As she tried to go to sleep, she tossed and turned thinking about the message on Uncle Haverson's house.

Had Joseph finally found her? Would this nightmare never end? Joseph was slapping her. Right cheek, left cheek, right cheek, left cheek. She ducked, and his fist connected with her solar plexus. She doubled over and prayed for it to end. Then an elephant came into the room and grabbed him by the neck and threw him into the nearby pond. What a relief! As she smiled broadly, she saw him crawling up to the shoreline. She began to run, and as she ran, she kept looking behind her. She looked forward and realized it was too late to stop her from going over a cliff. As she fell through the air, she waited for the impact and woke up to a soft landing on her bed. She had been dreaming, but besides the elephant, it had seemed so real. Sometimes she felt like killing herself because waiting for Joseph to do it was incredibly painful. She was so grateful that she was no longer living with Uncle Haverson. That had saved her life. She prayed, "Dear God, I'm so scared. What should I do? Joseph has found me, and I'm so confused. How could he have found me? Please show me what to do. I will trust you for whatever you have for my life. Thank you for keeping me safe. In Jesus's name. Amen."

Again, Joseph found himself waiting to use the washing machine. Someone was always taking his place in line. A large inmate with snake tattoos approached him. He believed his name was Tank. He bent down and whispered in his ear, "She wasn't there, but we left a message."

"What do you mean you painted my name in red letters on her uncle's house? What were you thinking? I wanted her brought to my house in New York. How hard can it be to bring one petite woman by boat to my bungalow?"

"What do you want me to do?"

"Find her! I want Phoebe! You want to hope that your mercenaries haven't scared her into hiding again."

"What is our next step?"

"I said FIND HER! God help you all if you can't find her in the two months I've got left in this joint!" Tank retreated as Joseph in his rage punched the washer and left a big dent in the side.

CHAPTER 15

Phoebe was depressed. It wasn't the weather, for every day in Natal was sunny, except for short afternoon showers. She had to shake herself out of it. It had been two weeks since the invasion at Uncle Haverson's house, but the nightly dreams about it kept it fresh. The blood kept flashing before her eyes. And what about Uncle's office? Where was it? She was startled by the sound of a truck's horn. It was late! She had twenty minutes to get to work, and she was still in her bathrobe. She didn't need to lose her job! She quickly got into a black and white skirt and shirt outfit, something she had designed herself just a month ago. The shoes were alligator, which had stirred quite a bit of controversy. Good controversy. Already, attention was drawn to her as a designer, and World Traders, a company in Paris, had tried to recruit her. She had smiled when she had received that letter. She had arrived at work and was paying for the taxi when she came back to the task at hand. The short walk up to her office gave her the much-needed time to compose herself because the thoughts of her new attention had brought back Phoebe's fear of Joseph. She couldn't let this rule her life. She wouldn't let this rule her life!

It wasn't until her noon break that she had time to adjust to the news and commitment she had made this morning. She was going to New York! She was going to face her fear. She had been recognized by a large design company in New York City, and they wanted her and Aware! to debut her summer line at their spring runway show. She felt on top of the world. She had to tell someone, and Uncle came to mind.

It rang only once, and Uncle picked up. "Phoebe, it is so good to hear from you! What's up?"

Silence. "Well, Uncle, I'm going to New York."

"Is that a good thing? Are you okay?"

She could tell by his questions that he was thinking about Joseph. His abuse had reached the very fiber of her family. "Not Joseph, Uncle. I'm being showcased at the city's most sought-after spring debut. Isn't that exciting?"

"It is if you think so. It seems kind of close to the last event if you ask me. Why don't you let me look into his whereabouts and get back to you in a couple of days."

She didn't have to think twice about it. "That would be great, Uncle! I don't leave until next Thursday. I'll call you this Saturday, and see if you know anything."

"Call me on Monday afternoon or evening, and I will have an answer then."

"I love you, Uncle."

"I love you too, little bird." Uncle got off the phone and immediately sat down. He was due to fly to England this week as a representative for the security council. They wanted him to be there, but he could send his plans with his assistant. It was too bad, but family came first. He didn't have to wonder about where Phoebe got her stubborn streak. She came by it rightly from her father. He touched his arm and noticed that one of the stab wounds had cut into one of the many scars he had received while working as an active agent. Sometimes he wished he could tell Phoebe everything.

CHAPTER 16

Tomorrow she would leave for New York. Phoebe had packed two days ago and, professionally, was more than ready. She did have her doubts when she thought of who she was being compared to, fashion designers from all over the country and some from abroad. Now the real moment of truth had come, the one she had dreaded for almost a week. She had to find out if Uncle could tell her about Joseph's whereabouts. Joseph, who still flooded her dreams with his angry face and handsome body. How could someone be so attracted to a man who had pummeled her soul and body? How many times had she gone back to him? Now, after years of being chased around the world, it had seemed like she had escaped his grasp here in Brazil, but once again he had found her or someone that knew his name had found her. It had been a close call. Her dread intensified as she picked up her cell phone. She thought the fear had intensified because she had had to wait so long. Initially, Uncle had said he would get back to her in two days, but then he had called and said that he needed a couple more days, that it was complicated.

Actually, it had taken his men exactly twenty-seven hours and twenty-three minutes to find Joseph. What took longer was finding out how long he was going to be in jail and how he was communicating with the outside. Exactly how he had arranged to find Phoebe in the first place? Uncle had thought of doing this before when the men attacked him and his house, but he had been preoccupied with a security breech in Scotland Yard. That had taken days of planning and weeks of implementation, but finally, the leak was found, and a top official was quietly taken care of. He was glad that he wasn't one of those who cleaned up the problems; it just wasn't his thing. He had succeeded in what he had sought to find out about Joseph. What he needed the extra time to do was to figure out what to tell Phoebe and how to clean up a mess that was his own investigation and not an official one.

Phoebe dialed Uncle and heard her heart pounding in her ears as the phone rang. "Hello, little bird. How's my favorite niece?"

"Okay, Uncle, but please don't make me wait. I need peace on this trip. I'm afraid."

"Sorry, honey. I just want you to relax because everything is going to be fine. Joseph is where he can't hurt you."

"What do you mean? Where is he?" There was a pregnant pause.

"He's in prison. He assaulted the wrong person and is doing a two-year sentence. He gets out shortly, but not before you are safely back here."

"Oh! Uncle, I'm so relieved! Uncle, do you know how Joseph found me in the first place?"

"I do know, but let me assure you I will keep you safe and no one can track you ever again. I will make sure of that."

"Uncle, I don't understand. Please tell me how or who helped find me? I need to know who I can trust."

"Phoebe, one man was responsible for Joseph finding you."

"Who? Please."

"It's been taken care of."

'Please, Uncle Haverson."

"It was the man who hired you at Aware! and your friend, Ralph Emerson."

CHAPTER 17

How could she go to New York now? Her boss and possibly the only man she had accepted male attention from in a very long time was dead. Uncle said it was taken care of discretely and probably wouldn't be discovered until well after she got back. How could she go when her future at Aware! was in question? After all, Ralph Emerson was the heart and soul of Aware! Where would they find a man or woman to take on the vision of their fashion center? There was no one on the horizon that even held a light to his leadership ability. But then, what better opportunity could she find in New York! What better place to showcase her talents and open herself up for another position. She had so many mixed feelings. She was sad because he was dead—confused as to why he would do this, curious as to how he was killed and who had arranged this, afraid of the forces of evil in general and of her future. What did the future hold for her? Despite the assurances from Uncle, she felt increased fear about Joseph's ability to reach her even from prison. The phone rang, and she jumped. The phone had been her enemy more than her friend. She didn't know if she could take anymore. She answered cautiously, "Hello?"

It was Uncle Haverson. "Phoebe, I know it's late and you're leaving tomorrow, but could you please come over to my house? I want to talk to you about something that I don't want to discuss over the phone."

"Sure, Uncle. If it's important to you, then it's important to me." Phoebe got dressed, called a taxi, and quickly went to the door. She waited in the secure lobby of her building while she waited for the taxi to arrive. She didn't have any time to think about what Uncle might want because on the ride over the taxi driver talked nonstop about whether she had heard that Natal was in the news today because of a fashion business that was being featured in New York City. In fact, he told her that she looked like the woman in the article. She really had not been listening, but when he had said that her ears had perked up, and she said, "What paper?"

He said, "Look for yourself. It's right here." There displayed on the front page of the Business News was a 5"×7" picture of her showing one of her summer line outfits. Her face displayed surprise, then pride, then fear. This was a major newspaper that would be seen by millions. She didn't have time for all of it to register as they had pulled up to Uncle's house. As she got out, she saw Uncle waiting for her on the doorstep with a different look on his face. She couldn't place the look. Maybe it was anxiety. Anyway, here she was, and she was hoping that it wouldn't take long because she really needed her rest for this trip. They settled in Uncle's new office, which was located where the spare bedroom used to be. This both surprised and confused Phoebe because she thought she wasn't allowed to be here or know its secrets.

He started right off, "Phoebe, I want you to know everything. What I really do for a living, how I know the things I know, and I want to tell you how I will keep you safe from danger for the rest of your life. Are you ready?"

She stared at him like she was seeing him for the first time. She responded quietly, "I think so."

CHAPTER 18

He started quickly like he wanted to get it over with. She had been waiting for this entrance to his life for a long time. "First of all, I want you to know that what I'm about to tell you may cause you a considerable amount of danger, but I will explain to you how I will keep you safe. I am the head of a division of security in the United States Government terrorist watch group. We specialize in cleaning up people or groups that threaten the security of our allies and their governments. I can keep you safe by assigning a team of experts to know every detail of your life and to protect you, very discreetly, from any danger to yourself or the ones you love. It is important for you to know that the president himself is the only one I answer to and that I didn't have clearance to tell you this information. I trust you to take it to your grave." She stared at him and wondered if this were really her uncle Haverson or an alien from outer space. She had so many questions racing through her mind, and the last statement about her grave had put a look of terror on her face. Uncle Haverson looked at Phoebe with concern and said, "Phoebe, are you okay? You look like you've seen a ghost or like you're about to pass out."

"No, I'm okay, Uncle. It's just that when you said I should take it to my grave that I thought about Joseph and how, twice, he beat me so bad that I thought I was dying. I really thought I was going to die. When you said grave, I pictured myself in a coffin because of Joseph."

"I'm sorry, Phoebe. Maybe I shouldn't have told you."

Phoebe quickly retorted, "No, no, Uncle! I wanted to know. I needed to know. Do you think it is still safe for me to go to New York? Will we still be able to see each other? Will I have to move frequently? Will my friends be in danger? I'm scared."

Uncle motioned with his hands up and down like a policeman trying to slow traffic approaching an accident. "Slow down! One thing at a time, Phoebe. It's very safe for you to go to New York. I've already taken care of the security for your trip. Where everyone that is going to the spring debut is on a guest list, I have had everyone investigated, and the girls working the runway just happen to have been cleared already by one of my subcontracted security companies. Any problems have been taken care of by arranging them to have a more pressing engagement with no one being hurt. They all have canceled."

"Well, how will I know who is my protection and who isn't?"

Uncle smiled. "You will have a 'boyfriend' traveling with you who will tell you everything."

Phoebe smiled cynically. "And how will I know who this 'boyfriend' is, huh?"

The door to the study opened and in walked a beautiful man. "Hi, I'm Mark, but you can call me Marcus."

CHAPTER 19

"Marcus? What kind of name is that? How do you expect him to know everything about me in twenty-four hours? And"—she thought with a chill—"what do you think Joseph would do if he thought I was with another man?" She felt panic rise in her throat.

"Phoebe, Joseph is taken care of. We have considered every angle, and his rats and informants are permanently gone." He paused, waiting to see if Phoebe had registered anything he had just said. Seeing a slight revelation in her face, Uncle continued, "Phoebe, have I not always been there for you? Don't you trust your uncle, your own flesh and blood?"

She stared into space, almost as if she had gone into shock. Her phone rang. Instead of being startled, she just stared at it. The tension in the room grew as the phone continued to ring.

Finally, Uncle asked Phoebe, "Aren't you going to answer it?"

She didn't move, and the ringing stopped.

Uncle began, "Phoebe, I know that lecturing you is not my style, but I think you need to hear something about your mother. This may be a shock to hear, but that is what I think you need right now." Phoebe looked at Uncle Haverson with interest in her eyes. "I know your mother left you when you were two years old, and you probably don't remember anything about your time with her, but I do. She met your father when she was just a young lady struggling to make it in the newspaper business in New York City. She finally began to really make it when she worked on a fashion column that no one else wanted to work on. She did it with a passion that I've often seen in your eyes when you talk about your fashion design work." Phoebe couldn't help herself, and she smiled. Uncle continued, "That's when things got rough for her with your father. He was the accountant at the *Journal*. It was bad from the start. He beat her from the very first date."

Phoebe put her hand over her mouth. She thought, *How could my father have done anything that bad?*

Uncle continued, "She left over and over again, but always went back at his promises to never do it again. Phoebe, don't let this happen to you. Don't let Joseph control your life anymore. You can make a fresh start. There's a man out there for you who will love you and respect you. You have to believe that you are worth that and that it really does exist." Phoebe had mixed feelings. She was glad that Uncle believed in her but very angry that her father, whom she had loved all her life, had been such a monster. Why hadn't he abused her stepmother too? Something didn't make sense.

Finally, she couldn't stand it any longer. She asked, "Uncle, how could you talk to your brother after what he did to my mother?" She couldn't call him her father anymore.

Uncle looked at the floor. Carefully choosing his words, he smiled at Phoebe, "My brother is not your father. At least in the physical sense. He stepped in when our agency got involved with an espionage case at the *Journal*, and your father was no longer able to take care of you." She looked really confused.

Uncle quickly explained, "Your mother left you because she feared for her life and was told by our agency that you would be taken care of, and as you do know, she was killed in an automobile accident, but your father—" Uncle couldn't say it.

Phoebe demanded, "Where is my father?"

Uncle sighed. "He was taken care of by the agency."

Marcus cleared his throat. Shifting his feet, he asked, "Do you still need my services, sir?"

CHAPTER 20

Phoebe couldn't believe it. So much had changed in the last twenty-four hours. She now knew everything about her family's history and how her mother had been abused by her father. She also, now, had real hope that she would break that cycle of abuse with the help of Uncle, who believed wholeheartedly in her, and a God that was becoming ever more real and personal to her. As for this Marcus who sat beside her on the plane, she just trusted that her uncle knew what he was doing when he had assigned him to take care of her security. The flight went without a hitch, and now they were landing at Kennedy Airport. There were two more professional-looking security personnel waiting for them in the airport, and the four of them were whisked away in a nondescript dark window sedan.

Phoebe found herself caught up in the excitement of the fashion show preparations. The girls were great, and everyone seemed to know exactly what they were supposed to be doing. Celeste, the stage manager and director, kept everything moving at a steady and orderly pace. The outfits Phoebe had created for the summer line looked great, even better on the girls that they had chosen to wear them. As for the security staff, even though they were everywhere, they were never in the way. It was actually comforting to see them. Marcus was always behind her, and that took Phoebe a while to get used to, but because her uncle had told her that it was necessary, she soon got used to it. Besides, she was too busy to think about it.

A bell went off, and Celeste yelled, "Thirty minutes until runway!" The girls and the many assistants, makeup artists, and fitters quickened their pace. "As for you, Phoebe, it is time for you and your security staff to leave backstage and be seated on the side of the runway. Remember, you will be called upon at the end of the show to come up the side stairs to be introduced to the audience. So remember where the stairs are, and pay attention to the woman over there in the green pantsuit who will appear on stage to introduce you. Now, off with you!" Celeste hurried away.

Phoebe felt put in her place, but it did not reduce the high she felt from what was happening. She was born for this! Marcus took her hand as they left backstage and went down the hallway leading to the side entrance to the auditorium. As they approached the door, they had an awkward moment deciding who should go first. Phoebe later couldn't remember who actually had. What she did remember was as the door opened, what should have been light was sudden enveloping darkness as she was pushed to the floor and covered with something, probably a dark cloth. Then, she felt rough hands carrying her. She heard men giving orders, but she really couldn't understand what they were saying because of the cloth and probably her shock. She was put in what sounded like a van with a comfortable rug on the floor. They didn't travel long, but during that time her mind was busy.

At first, she wondered, *Who has taken me? Then where is Marcus?* She was surprised at that and wondered if she was getting attached to him. She thought some more, *Would this be my ultimate end? Had Joseph finally succeeded? Would she join her mother in the great beyond?* Finally, she prayed, "Lord Jesus, I don't know my future, but I want to thank you for freeing me from the cycle of abuse and for blessing me with the opportunity to show my fashions in New York. Whatever happens, thank you. In Jesus's name. Amen."

The van stopped, and she was carried inside a building and set down gently on the floor. The cloth was unwrapped from her, and she slowly blinked her eyes to adjust to the light. There standing in front of her was a man. She cried out, "Uncle Haverson, it's you!"

CHAPTER 21

It was so dark. Phoebe couldn't see anything and wondered if her eyes were really open or not. Maybe she just thought her eyes were open. She could feel the darkness. Then in the distance, she saw a small light approaching her, and she realized she was on a mattress in the middle of a large rectangular room with cement walls and floors. Where was she? She pondered. As the light approached, her heart began to beat rapidly, but soon she realized it was her uncle Haverson. It came back to her in a rush. She had been abducted from the backstage of the spring fashion show in New York. What was going on? Uncle approached her slowly and tenderly. "Phoebe, how are you? How do you feel?" he asked.

She looked up at him and stared. What could she say? She didn't know where to begin. "Where am I?" Boy, that was a stupid question, she thought, but that was what came out.

"Honey, you're in one of the agency's protective warehouses. That's why there are no windows and very few lights. You've been through a lot, so perhaps I can give you a drink of something and you could get some more rest?"

"No way, Uncle, I know what you 'spy guys' put in people's drinks, and besides, I have lots of questions."

He pulled up a chair from out of the edges of the darkness and sat down. "Go ahead, I'm ready. Ask anything you want."

"Well, to begin with, what in the world happened back there at the show?"

"How far back do you want me to go?"

"All the way back."

"I'll make it as simple as possible." He lowered his voice for no apparent reason. "Before you left Brazil, we were following a lead that something was planned at the show. At the same time, another part of the agency was following many leads to planned threats on my life and the lives of my family. By coincidence, these two separate teams found themselves following the same trail and realized it all led to the fashion show in New York that we were both attending. Here is where it gets complicated. Joseph was stabbed yesterday in the prison bathroom and is now hanging on for his life in the intensive care unit of Beth Israel Hospital." Phoebe stared at her uncle. "Are you okay, honey?"

"Yes, Uncle. Please continue."

"It turns out that the man who assaulted him is a relative of Emerson's. When Emerson was killed, he wanted revenge on Joseph. He wanted revenge on me, the agency, and you, Phoebe."

"Me?"

"Yes, you. Joseph had pictures of you all over his cell, and this man had grown to hate everything you represented."

"Why did you grab me at the show?"

"We thought we had taken care of all the loose ends to their plan, but they were very smart, and they had other plans to engage in if the others were blocked. He is a very determined man. Thankfully, your uncle is a very smart man." Uncle smiled. "I always have an escape plan. That is what happened. Marcus, your security guard, didn't even know." Phoebe looked into the darkness and then back at Uncle's face. "Honey, little bird. What has you so frightened?"

"Uncle, where is Marcus?" Her heart was thundering, waiting for his response, expecting the worse.

"Phoebe," Marcus gently called her name from behind her. She then realized he was sitting in a chair not ten feet behind her in the darkness where she hadn't looked. She didn't know what overtook her, but she jumped up and walked quickly across the ten feet between them and muckled onto him as if he were saving her from drowning. She opened her eyes wide and looked at his face. "Oh, Marcus. I thought you were gone." In the dim light of the battery-powered lamp, she didn't see Uncle's big smile.

CHAPTER 22

Phoebe walked down the streets of Manhattan from outfitter to outfitter amazed at the number of her clothes that were in the windows and on the sidewalks. Since the fashion show where Uncle Haverson had saved her life, and her future, things had moved along rapidly. She later learned that in her absence, the show had still gone off beautifully. Uncle had prepared ahead of time a double who had gone on stage as her at the end of the show for the introduction of the designer. She had given the same speech that Phoebe had been prepared to give that Uncle had "borrowed" to read because he was curious. Phoebe laughed at a sophisticated spy using that lame excuse.

Phoebe had later seen pictures of her double introduced as "New York City's Up and Coming" and didn't feel too disappointed because she was very charming. Uncle said Phoebe was more charming of course and could never be adequately substituted. Phoebe and Marcus had begun a casual dating experience, but nothing too serious. Phoebe just really liked him, and the feeling was mutual. Her new job in the city was in design development at New York's Regional School of Design in Manhattan. It involved being one of the movers and shakers behind what was taught or not at the school, and she was allowed all the resources the school had to develop and expand her continuing line of specialty clothing. She spent some of her free time volunteering at the New York Domestic Violence Hotline in its Manhattan office, something her counselor and Marcus had encouraged her to do. Phoebe had come a long way since Joseph's death, but it seemed like her issues never ended.

The PTSD (post-traumatic stress disorder) that she suffered from as a result of her intensely abusive relationship with Joseph made it difficult to trust or be intimate with others. It had been a difficult decision to make, when Joseph died, to not go to his funeral. She would never forget the date—May 12. Against Uncle Haverson's advice, she had spent the day alone in her apartment in Natal, Brazil, looking at pictures of herself and Joseph. Sometimes she cried, and sometimes she laughed. Once in a while, she would take a picture and rip it to shreds. When she got to the end of the last photo album, she felt an incredible rage as she looked at the picture of herself standing next to Joseph in Times Square. He looked so handsome, yet so overpowering, and she looked so pale and wore a fake smile. On the right side of her face, near her eye, she could see the shadow of a large bruise that she had tried to cover with makeup. She remembered that one clearly. It was her punch in the face for calling an old friend whom Joseph had made clear to her that she was to have no contact with.

Her friend's name was Alicia, and when Phoebe later moved to New York, Alicia connected her with resources and a counselor to help her to heal. On top of being Phoebe's workout partner at the gym, Alicia was also a volunteer on the hotline where Phoebe worked. Phoebe and Alicia met together once in a while with another girl, Amanda, who was still struggling with what to do in her abusive relationship. In the closing chapters of Phoebe's journey of remembering Joseph, she pulled every photo of Joseph out of the photo albums and put them in a large metal trash can, took them outside into the beautiful sunshine of Natal, and burned every last one of them. May 12 was the day that Phoebe started a new photo album. The first picture she put in it was a picture of herself at church in fourth grade receiving her first Bible from the minister. She wavered for a moment, then took the latest picture she had and put that next to it. Looking at the picture of Marcus in his jeans and sweater, Phoebe rested her head back on the loveseat and a sweet look of contentment came over her face.

CHAPTER 23

Moving to Manhattan had brought about big changes for Phoebe. First, the new apartment was smaller, and then there was the job. It consumed all of her time and although she loved every minute of it, there was little time for a social life, let alone cleaning her apartment. She could afford a maid, so she hired one. Nuvia was a beautiful young woman from Guatemala, and she loved to talk. Often Phoebe would stop by home to pick up something, and because of Nuvia's compassionate listening and sharing, Phoebe would find it hard to leave. Counseling was overwhelming sometimes, and she wondered if it was worth it. She felt angrier and angrier all the time. If it weren't for her workouts with Alicia, she felt she would explode. Once when she was on the phone at the domestic violence call center, she had gotten so angry that she had had to excuse herself and get another volunteer to take over, saying (falsely) that her shift was over.

One day when she was shopping at Walmart, she saw a man pulling forcefully on his girlfriend's arm while she was trying to get away. It was then that the nightmares began. She would find herself waking up in a drenching sweat with Joseph standing over her with his fist raised ready to punch her, and when she flinched, she would wake up from the dream within the dream. Sometimes she would wake up only to find herself in a dream, and then it became a dream inside a dream. Phoebe sometimes felt like she spent the whole night trying to get away from that punishing fist of Joseph. When she woke up for real, she would be sore all over and would wonder if Joseph was in the apartment and had really beat her. It seemed so real, without telling Marcus why she would sometimes ask him to stay at the apartment overnight, stating that it made her feel safer. Well, really it did. One night that Marcus stayed over, she was awakened by Marcus shaking her. It was especially frightening because in the dream, Joseph had been whipping her head back and forth like a rag doll. When Phoebe awakened, she stared at Marcus with her big brown eyes like she was seeing a ghost. Marcus had asked her what was wrong and told her that she had been screaming. Phoebe didn't tell him what was going on because she wasn't sure herself. She realized then that she needed to do something because their lovemaking was in trouble. She found herself unable to respond to Marcus's touch. She let him do all the work, just like when Joseph raped her. She said, "I'm just out of the habit." The problem was that the more Phoebe dealt with her Joseph issues, the more messed up her life was getting. Looking at the ceiling and imagining the poor children of Afghanistan was the only way she got through Marcus's grunts and groans. What was she going to do? She called her dad in Connecticut.

CHAPTER 24

Phoebe's dad answered the phone on the first ring. "Phoebe, my love, it's been so long. What's up?" Phoebe opened her mouth to explain and all that came out were sobs and sobs. "Phoebe, honey, you go right ahead and cry. I know the answer to your problem."

Phoebe snapped out of her crying in a rage. "You don't know anything! I'm a mess. My whole life is perfect, and I'm a wreck."

"Is Marcus giving you a hard time?"

"No, Dad. It's me. Everything is me. I'm ruining everything."

"Who told you this, Phoebe. Who told you that you're ruining everything?"

Phoebe spoke softly, "I guess I did. Oh, Dad, I'm so scared. You see, Marcus and I are getting kind of serious, and all I keep seeing is Joseph. I think I might even love him."

"Have you told Marcus what's going on with you?"

"No, Dad. I don't want to lose the best relationship with a man that I've ever had."

"Do you want my advice?"

Phoebe laughed (more of a girlish giggle). "Why do you think I called you?"

"To yell at me?"

"No and yes. No, I didn't call you to yell at you, and, yes, I want your advice."

There was a pregnant pause. "Well, Phoebe, if Marcus means that much to you, then tell him the truth."

"What if it drives him away?"

Another pause. "Honey, if he runs from you, then he was never the man you thought he was. And Phoebe, pray. Your heavenly Father can solve any loneliness that may result from his leaving. But if I know Marcus, you are well worth the wait while you figure this all out."

"Thanks, Dad. I am always forgetting to pray, but God is always there for me when I need Him. By the way, how would you know about Marcus? I've probably only mentioned him twice in my letters." Phoebe reacted with suspicion.

Her father laughed for almost as long as she had cried at the onset of their call. "You're asking that from a man whose brother is a spy."

Phoebe laughed and then suddenly stopped. "Are you saying that you're keeping tabs on me? You guys are out of control!" She felt her anger rising.

"Phoebe, honey, I only followed Haverson's investigation in the initial phases to make sure you wouldn't get hurt in any way. I love you. The fact that I know he has brown hair and blue eyes, is six foot, four inches tall, and weighs 226 pounds is because I read his identification cover sheet. I promise. I'm done. I will not stick my nose in your business. I will trust you to God's protection, just like I'm hoping you will trust this relationship you two have to God."

"Thanks, Dad! You're the best dad ever!" The doorbell rang. "Oh, that must be Marcus. Dad, pray!"

"You pray too, honey."

"I will, bye."

"Bye."

The doorbell rang again. "Hold on, Marcus, I'll be right there." Phoebe went quickly to her bedroom and knelt beside her bed. "Jesus, I've been ignoring you a lot lately. I know you're here in the good times as well as the bad times, and this is one of them. Help me be honest with Marcus and help me to accept what happens, even losing Mar"— Phoebe sniffled and said it again—"even losing Marcus. Amen." She wiped her tears away and got up quickly and walked softly to the door. She opened the door wide and smiled at his sober-looking face.

He looked at her with concern. "Have you been crying?" She nodded yes. "Well, I have come to cheer you up. I have big news!" Marcus quickly apologized, "I'm sorry, Phoebe. Do you want to talk about it?"

"Not yet, Marcus, maybe later."

CHAPTER 25

She had to stop him. Letting Marcus go on and propose to her, as she sensed he was about to do, would be a lie, and then how could she back out or hurt this man whom she loved. Phoebe yelled, "Stop, you can't, you don't understand!"

"Phoebe, what's wrong? Tell me. What don't I understand?"

"Everything… I…" Phoebe tried, but all that came out was sobs. He rushed to her side, but she held him off at arm's length. "Let me do this," she continued. "I haven't been truly honest with you. I've been asking you to spend nights because I'm afraid. It might sound foolish, but I'm afraid of being alone. Joseph keeps visiting me at night and beating me. I know it's not real, but it seems like it. And even worse, when we have sex most of the time, I can't block out the image of Joseph raping me. I'm sorry, Marcus. I think I'm too much of a mess for you." Phoebe gently put her face in her hands and wept her whole body shaking with sobs

Gently, Marcus took Phoebe's hands away from her face and held them tenderly between his. "Phoebe, I've not been honest with you either. I sometimes see myself in bed with another man." Marcus waited for that to sink in.

Phoebe stared right through him for a moment then looked him straight in the eye and whispered, "Another man?"

"Yes, Phoebe another man. You see, my first sexual encounters for years were through being molested by neighborhood boys. You're only the second woman I've ever been with. You see, we both have hurdles to climb over. But I'm working with a Christian counselor who believes in me, and I hope you will continue counseling, and together, God can heal us." Marcus finished with hope in his voice.

Phoebe squeezed his hands and said, "Marcus, if you'll have this, then I'll have your mess," and she smiled.

"I haven't even proposed yet," Marcus snapped back. They grabbed one another and fell on the carpet in an embrace. They kissed as if they had never kissed before and decided this needed to be finished in the bedroom where they wouldn't bump into the furniture.

The next morning came quickly, and they both realized that something magical had taken place. They looked each other in the eye and gave each other the sweetest bad morning breath kiss ever.

CHAPTER 26

The trip to Connecticut was taking longer than she thought it would, but she was enjoying the fall foliage immensely. It was gorgeous, and the blends of oranges, reds, and yellows did much to still her busy mind. It had been almost eight years since her last trip here. It wasn't that she hadn't wanted to see her father and stepmother, but she got so wrapped up in Joseph that she had forgotten the warm, loving home where she had been raised. She drove off the exit following the signs to the University of Connecticut. It was as if the town of Storrs, where it was located, didn't exist outside of the campus. She turned down Gurleyville Road and at the bottom of the hill turned right onto Chaffeeville. So many memories flooded her mind as thoughts of people she had been friends with, who were now gone, entered her mind. She felt the energy of her youth surge within her as she approached the turn onto Wildwood Road. She had spent many hours waiting at the bus stop with the other kids, and they had played tricks on passing cars by holding an invisible rope across the road. The hill up Wildwood was just as steep as she remembered. She recalled the exact spot where her father had given up trying to teach her standard shift in his AMC Gremlin.

Later, he had hired a young man to teach her the ropes. He had become her first boyfriend, but that flame quickly went out. As she approached the house, she was surprised by all the new houses that had sprouted up since her last time here. They had even replaced the wooden bridge over the brook with a modern-looking steel thing. Dad and Joan were expecting her. Phoebe had called a week ago to say she needed to see them. They were relieved to hear from her and calmed her fears of rejection by assuring her that that was her home and she could stay as long as she wanted to. An unfamiliar dog came running out to meet her rental car as she entered the driveway. She realized a lot had changed. The little black and tan mutt wagged its tail and acted as if Phoebe was a part of the family. Dad had to rescue her from his affections. After picking up the dog, he approached Phoebe tentatively, and once she met his advances, he gave her a bear hug that was only interrupted by Joan running out to meet her. Joan looked younger than her years and had lost a few pounds. Phoebe was relieved to see that she was still the rotund, happy woman she remembered so fondly. She recalled how she had helped Phoebe to adjust to calling her Joan when Phoebe had become older. Joan had insisted on it, assuring Phoebe that it would keep that special "Mom" place for her birth mother. She told Phoebe it was what her mother would have wanted. There was nothing to stop their embrace, and soon she found herself crying tears of joy, sadness, fear, and relief. It was as if a river poured out of her. Finally, Phoebe held her at arm's length and smiled like the sun. "Dad, Joan. I'm getting married!"

SUGGESTED BOOK LIST

Foland, Constance M. *A Song for Jeffrey*.
Fowler, Connie May Fowler. *Before Women Had Wings*.
The Holy Bible
Kidd, Sue Monk. *The Secret Life of Bees*.
Lamb, Wally. *She's Come Undone*.
Martel, Yann, *Life of Pi*.

SPECIAL THANKS

I want to thank all the people who have made this book possible.

To my family and friends who have supported me in countless ways including listening to me talk about this book; helping me with technology issues and document questions; reading over many drafts of the "Book Summary," "About the Author," "Dedication," and "Special Thanks" and giving their opinions; supporting this project financially; telling me how much they are proud of me; and most importantly rejoicing with me.

To all the local, state, national, and international hotline workers who willingly and compassionately answered questions about resources for the women and men needing assistance.

To my Christian sisters in Canada and Mexico who readily helped me to verify the domestic violence resources in those countries

To my Lord and Savior, Jesus Christ, who gave me His Holy Spirit to empower me to write and prepare this story for printing and who put this book in your hands.

Lastly, to the staff at Covenant Books who, from start to finish, have been patient with this first-time author who didn't even own a computer, helping me to bring this story to print.

Thank you all!

ABOUT THE AUTHOR

The author lives in Maine, where she enjoys writing and spending time with her family and friends. Her passion for writing began in middle school, where she wrote mostly poems at first. Over the years, she has expanded into writing stories, writing in journals, and now writing books. It is her heart's desire to bring enjoyment to her readers and inspiration to new authors, young and old alike, that they may find the courage to launch their writings into the public arena.

www.ingramcontent.com/pod-product-compliance
Lightning Source LLC
Chambersburg PA
CBHW022111150726
47990CB00003B/1324